CW00383206

# The Battle of Britain Story

# The Battle of Britain Story

Graham Pitchfork

The
History
Press

Published in the United Kingdom in 2010 by
The History Press
The Mill · Brimscombe Port · Stroud · Gloucestershire · GL5 2QG

Reprinted 2017

Copyright © Graham Pitchfork, 2010

All rights reserved. No part of this publication may be
reproduced, stored in a retrieval system, or transmitted, in any
form, or by any means, electronic, mechanical, photocopying,
recording or otherwise, without the prior permission of the
publisher and copyright holder.

Graham Pitchfork has asserted his moral right to be identified as
the author of this work.

British Library Cataloguing in Publication Data
A catalogue record for this book is available from the British
Library.

ISBN 978-0-7524-5682 9

Typesetting and origination by
The History Press
Printed and bound in China.

**Half title page:** *A Spitfire engages a Messerschmitt Bf 109.*

**Title page:** *Vapour trails.*

# CONTENTS

# ACKNOWLEDGEMENTS

Over the years, much of my research of the RAF's unique history has been carried out at the Air Historical Branch, where Sebastian Cox – the Head of the Branch – and Graham Day have always been very helpful, and at the National Archives where I am grateful for advice from Catherine Bradley and William Spencer.

Group Captain Patrick Tootal and Geoff Simpson of the Battle of Britain Memorial Trust have been very supportive and have allowed me to use some of their photographs. Others who have also permitted me to use their photographs are the 247 Squadron Association, 616 Squadron Association, the Aircrew Association, Ian Burrows of the Royal Observer Corps Historical Collection, Alan Carlaw of the 602 Squadron Association, Laurie Chester, Mike Dean, Ken Ellis – editor of *Flypast*, Chris Goss, Jeff Jefford, Glen Moreman, Roy Nesbit, Bob Ogley, Andrew Thomas, Tangmere Air Museum, Brian Waite of the 609 Squadron Association, Keith Woodcock and the Yorkshire Air Museum.

At The History Press, I would like to thank Amy Rigg, whose idea this book was, and Jennifer Younger.

▼ *RAF pilot's badge.*

The Battle of Britain was the first battle in history to be decided solely by air power. Described by many as the greatest air battle in history, it had a profound effect on the progress – and outcome – of the Second World War. With German domination of Europe following the fall of France, all that stood between defeat and survival for the Western World was Royal Air Force Fighter Command.

For centuries, the security of Great Britain's island status had been based on the Royal Navy's command of the surrounding seas. Apart from the scattered bombing raids by Zeppelins and Gotha bombers in the First World War, there had been nothing to threaten Britain's general population. The advent of the long-range bomber, however, changed the face of warfare: the whole nation became part of the front line.

In the years leading up to 1939, the Luftwaffe had built up a formidable capability. Following its swift and easy victories in Poland and Scandinavia, as well as the *Blitzkreig* into the Low Countries and France, Hitler and his air force commander, Generalfeldmarschall Hermann Goering, believed that the Luftwaffe would soon overwhelm the Royal Air Force and gain superiority of the skies, thus paving the way for an invasion across the English Channel. However, little thought had been given to planning an aerial campaign against Britain, and the Luftwaffe's intelligence organisation repeatedly underestimated the strength and capability of the Royal Air Force. It also grossly misjudged the skill of its commanders and the will of the general population of Britain.

**Did you know?**
The Observer Corps was established in 1925 and came under the control of the RAF in 1929. The Corps played a key role in the reporting of enemy aircraft, and its observers often spent hours in sand-bagged dugouts day and night.

A review of the conduct of the campaign highlights the contrasts between the respective higher commanders. Their personalities could hardly have been more different. Air Chief Marshal Sir Hugh Dowding, who had created an air defence system incorporating scientific developments that proved to be very effective, had a clear vision of his task and did not waver even when placed under great pressure – both political and service. He followed the crucial principle of war; the selection of an aim and the maintenance of it in a ruthless and unwavering manner. The vain, egotistical and grossly over-confident Goering, who often refused to accept the sound advice of his very capable senior commanders, fighter and bomber leaders, was in stark contrast. His inadequate directing of the Luftwaffe's campaign and the failures of his intelligence service proved to be a key factor in the RAF's ultimate victory.

Hitler and Goering also grossly under-estimated the resilience of the British people. Hitler had always anticipated that once he had conquered the rest of Europe, and the might of the Luftwaffe became apparent, then the British would sue for peace. With Churchill as Prime Minister this was never going to be an option whilst the RAF could keep the Luftwaffe at bay.

Victory in the Battle of Britain will always be synonymous with the 2,936 gallant RAF aircrew immortalised as 'The Few'. However, the part played by their highly professional, equally gallant and loyal ground crew and others should never be forgotten. So should not the efforts of those who served with Anti-

Aircraft and Balloon Commands, the men of the Observer Corps in their crude and uncomfortable outposts, the Home Guard, and the many others involved in the fire, rescue and medical services. The workers in the aircraft factories and other industries made prodigious efforts to increase their output so that Fighter Command always had enough fighters – just. Women played a major role, not only with the Women's Auxiliary Air Force (WAAF), but also in many of the civil organisations. Finally, whilst the fighter pilots fought their defensive battles in the skies of south-east England in full view of the population, the men of the Bomber and Coastal Commands played a crucial – if largely unnoticed – role in the counter-offensive, including attacks against invasion targets and centres of production as well as keeping the sea lanes open.

◄ Air Chief Marshal Sir Hugh Dowding, Commander-in-Chief of Fighter Command.

◄ *Ground crew of No.222 Squadron pose on a Spitfire.*

◄◄ *Pilots of No.601 (County of London) Squadron around one of their Hurricanes.*

However, all of these important supporting roles would have counted for nothing if the aircrew of Fighter Command had failed. Armies and navies on both sides of the Channel could do little but watch as a few thousand young men fought it out in the skies of England. Their victory ensured the survival of freedom and sent a clear message to the rest of the world: tyranny had to be defeated.

◄ *Young ATS women at a gun site with a range finder.*

As the 1930s progressed and Adolf Hitler rose to power in Germany, many began to realise that his regime posed a serious threat to world peace. Although banned by the Treaty of Versailles, which had been signed in June 1919, Germany had secretly been laying down the foundations of an air arm during the mid-1920s. The development of civil flying, including the establishment of the national airline, Lufthansa, and of gliding schools, encouraged a sense of air-mindedness and provided a nucleus of proficient pilots and ground engineers. By 1933 the aircraft industry was experimenting with military types, and in 1934 these began to appear in production. Within eighteen months over 4,000 aircraft had been produced, most of which were trainers.

In March 1935, Hitler and his Air Minister, Hermann Goering, a First World War fighter ace, felt sufficiently secure to proclaim to the world the foundation of the German Air Force – the Luftwaffe. Goering was appointed its Commander-in-Chief, and the units that had been concealed as 'flying clubs' were handed over to the Luftwaffe. By the end of 1935 the new air arm could muster almost 2,000 aircraft and some 20,000 officers and men.

The rapid rise of the Luftwaffe was noted with concern by the British Government, and in July 1934 the Prime Minister, Stanley Baldwin, announced an expansion of the Home Defence Air Forces from fifty-two to seventy-five squadrons, and for additions to the RAF to bring its worldwide strength up to 128 squadrons within five years. This became known as

*Generalfeldmarschall Hermann Goering, head of the Luftwaffe.*

*The crest of Fighter Command.*

 *The Hurricane prototype.*

Expansion Scheme 'A', and in the years leading up to the Second World War it was revised numerous times.

To reflect the demands of the RAF's expansion the Metropolitan Air Force was reorganised into four functional commands, thus Fighter Command – with its headquarters at Stanmore – was born. Its Commander-in-Chief was Air Marshal Sir Hugh Dowding. The fifty-four-year-old Dowding had previously commanded the RAF Inland (Fighter) Area before becoming Air Member for Supply and Research. It was this latter appointment that gave him the insight into, and knowledge of, research and scientific development.

Dowding was one of the first to recognise the potential danger of a rearming Germany, and he was acutely aware of the limitations of the RAF and the fact that his meagre fighter force would be no match for the emerging Luftwaffe. In response he set about creating an integrated air defence system. Dowding's Command consisted of two Fighter Groups: No.11, primarily for the defence of London, and No.12, for the defence of the eastern approaches across the North Sea. The civilian-manned Observer Corps completed his organisation.

Dowding's fighter squadrons were still in the bi-plane era. Equipped with just twin Vickers .303 machine guns, and with limited range, they posed little threat to an adversary equipped with heavily armoured fast bombers. Fortunately, two monoplane fighters had recently made their maiden flights, and the outstanding Hawker Hurricane and Supermarine Spitfire, equipped with radio and with their eight wing-mounted machine guns,

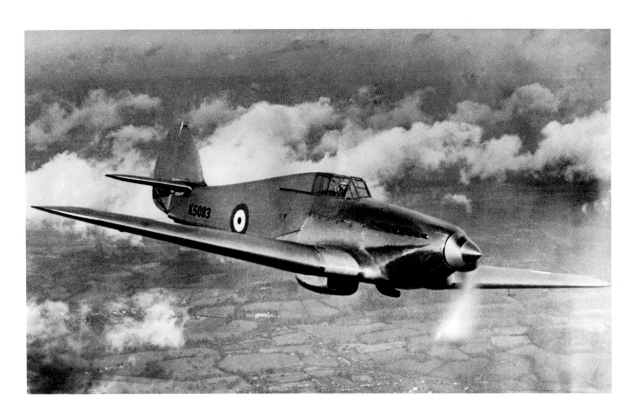

15

➤ *One of the Chain Home radar stations completed on the east and south coasts by 1940.*

would soon start to enter service with RAF squadrons.

Dowding's air defence system needed to be able to locate hostile aircraft quickly. During his time as Air Member for Research and Development, Dowding pressed for financial support for Robert Watson-Watt's work on developing a radio direction finding (RDF) aid. Approval was given in 1936 to construct the RDF stations, the first being erected to cover the approaches to London and the Thames. A chain of twenty stations was approved and built, each with a 250ft-high mast. In due course this was further expanded, and by 1940 a complete chain had been established, and was operational along the entire southern and eastern coasts of Great Britain.

In November 1938, the Secretary of State for Air, Sir Kingsley Wood, announced

to Parliament the last of the pre-war expansions of the RAF. Scheme 'M' planned to raise the Metropolitan Air Force to 163 squadrons (2,549 first-line aircraft), with an all-heavy Bomber Command of 85 squadrons and a Fighter Command of 50 squadrons. This new emphasis on the fighter arm was the scheme's distinguishing feature. Sir Kingsley Wood stated, 'I propose to give the highest priority to the strengthening of our fighter force, that force which is designed to meet the invading bomber in the air'. Thus the dictum 'the bomber will always get through' was overturned.

Central to Dowding's air defence system was early warning provided by the chain of RDF (now called radar) sites, with fifty-one individual posts each linked to Fighter Command Headquarters at Bentley Priory. From the coast it was the responsibility of the 30,000-strong all-volunteer Observer Corps – manning more than 1,000 posts – to track and plot enemy forces overland and feed information into Fighter Command and Group Operations Rooms. The Command was organised into four Groups, Nos 10, 11, 12 and 13, and for tactical control purposes each was divided into sectors based on a main fighter station with one or more satellite airfields with squadrons based on them.

The key to the effectiveness of the system was the concept of control. Central to this was the ability to simultaneously display the same information from the Operations Room at Dowding's headquarters at Bentley Priory to each sector controller. This created great flexibility, including the rapid transfer of reinforcements from one Group to another. In order that duplication

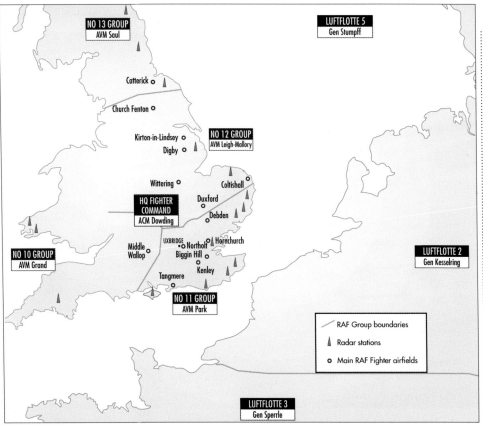

NO 13 GROUP
AVM Saul

LUFTFLOTTE 5
Gen Stumpff

Catterick ○

Church Fenton ○

Kirton-in-Lindsey ○

NO 12 GROUP
AVM Leigh-Mallory

Digby ○

Wittering ○

Coltishall ○

Duxford
○

HQ FIGHTER
COMMAND
ACM Dowding

Debden
○

UXBRIDGE
● Northolt
Hornchurch
○

Middle
Wallop ○

Biggin Hill ○

NO 10 GROUP
AVM Grand

Kenley ○

LUFTFLOTTE 2
Gen Kesselring

Tangmere ○

NO 11 GROUP
AVM Park

RAF Group boundaries

▲ Radar stations

○ Main RAF Fighter airfields

LUFTFLOTTE 3
Gen Sperrle

◄ *Position of Fighter Command headquarters and airfields and Luftwaffe air fleets.*

◄◄ *Two members of the Observer Corps manning the Gower Street K1 post.*

19

➤ *The Fighter Command Operations Room at Bentley Priory.*

**Did you know?**
The Rolls-Royce Merlin engine powered both the Hurricane and the Spitfire. It had been developed during the inter-war years as a private venture. This outstanding engine also powered the Lancaster bomber.

and mixing of friendly and hostile radar plots was eliminated, a 'filter' room was established. Trials and airborne exercises slowly refined the Dowding system and it proved to be a crucial element in future air battles. The success of the system relied on a complex network of telephone lines, and the General Post Office, a key component from the outset of its development, continued to play a crucial role in its ultimate success.

The Expansion Schemes of the late 1930s also created other major capabilities that would prove to be decisive when war broke out. Many new airfields were built, with twenty fighter airfields established by the outbreak of war. The introduction of the RAF Volunteer Reserve allowed for the training of pilots and ground crew to rapidly expand. The Auxiliary Air Force was increased and it is worthy to note that of the sixty-six RAF squadrons that flew during the Battle, fourteen were Auxiliaries.

◄ *No.616 (South Yorkshire) Squadron was one of fourteen Auxiliary Air Force Squadrons that fought in the Battle.*

Throughout the summer of 1939 war seemed inevitable, and on 24 August some reservists were called up and the Auxiliary Air Force was embodied into the RAF. Finally, on 1 September Hitler's forces attacked Poland and, three days later, Great Britain was at war with Germany.

*▼ Hurricane pilots at readiness.*

Four squadrons of Hurricanes were immediately sent to France, and over the next few months of the so-called 'Phoney War' others were sent as reinforcements. In April 1940, the German invasion of Norway took two fighter squadrons from Dowding's Command, both of which were destroyed. At dawn on 10 May the Germans launched their *Blitzkreig* and invaded the Low Countries. Two days later Winston Churchill became Prime Minister, promising further support to the French.

Fierce air fighting took place and Dowding was ordered to replace the heavy loss of fighters. On 16 May he felt compelled to write to the Under Secretary of State for Air, Harold Balfour, to express his deep concern following orders to send further fighter reinforcements to France. He pointed out that it had previously

*Pilots of No.87 Squadron rush to their Hurricanes at an airfield in northern France.*

**Did you know?**
The great majority of RAF fighters were equipped with the Browning .303 machine gun, which was capable of firing up to 1,260 rounds per minute.

been agreed that fifty-two squadrons were necessary for the defence of the United Kingdom, but he now had only thirty-six available. He wished to know how many squadrons were to be kept at home and concluded that, if his force was further drained away, the result would be 'the final, complete and irredeemable defeat of this country'. The Chief of the Air Staff, Air Chief Marshal Sir Cyril Newall, supported Dowding's brave stance, and no more fighters were sent to France.

The evacuation of the British Expeditionary Force began from the beaches of Dunkirk on 26 May. RAF fighters provided support, but the Battle of France resulted in the loss of almost twenty-five per cent of Fighter Command's strength; 432 Hurricanes and Spitfires. Equally as important was the loss of pilots, the great majority having been regular officers, including squadron and flight commanders. Fighting continued and the last of the RAF units did not return to England until 18 June. Over the following few weeks Dowding built up his depleted squadrons and trained new pilots, but the loss of experience could not be replaced so quickly.

As it became clear that Great Britain stood alone against Germany, the Prime Minister, Winston Churchill, broadcast to the nation:

What has been called the Battle of France is over. I expect the Battle of Britain to begin…Let us therefore brace ourselves to our duties, and so bear ourselves that, if the British Empire and its Commonwealth last for a thousand years, men will say, 'This was their finest hour.'

## BRITAIN ALONE

The six weeks of respite after the evacuation from the Dunkirk beaches proved a godsend to the RAF and the other services. Photographic reconnaissance and coastal patrols monitored the build up of German forces on the continent, and it soon became apparent that any invasion of the country was likely to be directed at the beaches in the south-east of England.

By the beginning of July, Dowding had fifty-four operational squadrons equipped with almost 1,000 aircraft, but only 600 were available for operations. Two of the squadrons were equipped with the Defiant and six with Blenheims, the latter mainly employed in the night-fighter role. They were organised into four Groups: twenty-two in Air Vice-Marshal Keith Park's No.11 Group in the south-east; fourteen in No.12 Group, which was commanded by Air Vice-Marshal Trafford Leigh-Mallory; fourteen in Air Vice-Marshal Richard Saul's No.13

◄ *Air Vice-Marshal Keith Park, Air Officer Commanding No.11 Group.*

➤ *Barrage balloons over central London.*

**Did you know?**
The Home Guard was formed in May 1940 when it was called the Local Defence Volunteer.

Group in the north of England and Scotland; and lastly, a new Group in the south-west of England, No.10 commanded by Air Vice-Marshal Sir Quintin Brand, which had just four at this stage. Dowding had strategic control of all Fighter Command's assets and he was responsible for the balloon barrage through the fighter groups. He also exercised general control of the other key elements in the air defence of Great Britain, the anti-aircraft guns and searchlights.

The replacement of aircraft lost during the debacle in France was a pressing issue. Winston Churchill appointed the press baron, Lord Beaverbrook, to run the newly created Ministry of Aircraft Production, and his robust manner and vigorous approach soon started to pay dividends as the output of new and repaired fighters rose steadily. Dowding's other major concern was the replacement of pilots. Volunteers were called for, with about fifty responding from the Fleet Air Arm, and some were transferred from the other RAF Commands, in particular the Army Co-operation Command.

## THE LUFTWAFFE

As the RAF made its preparations, the powerful Luftwaffe re-deployed and moved into position ready to destroy it. Commanded by Generalfeldmarschall Hermann Goering, soon to be promoted to Reichmarschall, it had gained considerable experience with its Condor Legion during the Spanish Civil War, which had broken out in 1936. This war provided a training ground for the new aircraft as well as combat experience for its pilots and aircrew, which proved invaluable in Germany's

**Did you know?**
The Bristol Blenheim aircraft was originally designed in 1933 to meet the requirement for a civil-commercial light-transport aircraft.

➤ *A Junkers Ju 87B Stuka dive-bomber.*

victorious campaigns in Poland, Norway and Western Europe in 1939 and the spring of 1940.

However, the Luftwaffe that confronted Fighter Command in the summer of 1940 was designed to support the army, not to fight a long-range war on its own. Also, blind faith in the *Blitzkrieg* tactics had created a high level of overconfidence and the expectation that the badly mauled RAF would soon be destroyed, thus creating the necessary conditions for the invasion of Great Britain. The German High Command saw the English Channel as a wide river, with the dive-bomber, the Junkers 87 Stuka playing the same key role as in earlier campaigns.

By early July, huge Air Fleets (*Luftflotten*) faced eastern and southern Britain from Norway in the north to the Atlantic Coast in Brittany. The largest, *Luftflotte* 2 commanded by Generalfeldmarschall Albert Kesselring, was deployed in the Pas de Calais region of northern France, a mere 100 miles from London. *Luftflotte* 3, under the command of Generalfeldmarschall Hugo Sperrle, was based in the north and west of France, and the total strength of these two Air Fleets amounted to about 1,200 long-range bombers, 400 dive-bombers and 1,100 fighters. *Luftflotte* 5 was based in Norway and Denmark, and was commanded by Generaloberst Hans-Jurgen Stumpf.

The task of these *Luftflotten* was to clear the Straits of Dover and to blockade Great Britain by attacking ports and shipping, in conjunction with mining operations against sea lanes and harbour entrances. A crucial task was to achieve air superiority over the RAF in preparation for the Operation

*Generalfeldmarschall Albert Kesselring, Commander of Luftflotte 2.*

*Seelöwe* (Sealion), the invasion of southern England.

## THE BATTLE – FIRST PHASE (10 JULY– 7 AUGUST)

Although the Luftwaffe had probed at British defences during the early days of July and many combats had taken place, most historians recognise 10 July as the opening of the first phase of the Battle of Britain – the *Kanalkampf*, or Channel Battle – when the Luftwaffe attacked Channel convoys and ports on the south coast. These attacks fell in the No.11 Group area, which had its headquarters at Uxbridge.

On the opening day, bomber formations, escorted by Messerschmitt Bf 109s and Bf 110s, attacked a convoy in the Straits of Dover, and another force caused damage in Swansea and Falmouth. RAF pilots noted with interest how quickly the Bf 110s went into a defensive circle once they were attacked by Hurricanes, indicating an inherent weakness in the aircraft's capability that would become even more apparent in the days ahead.

Another early observation was the scale of the Luftwaffe's air-sea rescue capability, highlighting a stark contrast with that of the RAF. Thirty Heinkel 59 seaplanes were available to land on the water and pick up airmen shot down into the sea. German pilots had inflatable rubber dinghies and a chemical that stained the sea. The British had no comparable system until February 1941. As a temporary measure, twelve Lysanders were borrowed from Army Co-operation Command to search for pilots and guide launches and other craft to the rescue. Unfortunately, RAF pilots were not equipped with a dinghy and many were lost before rescue arrived.

With no peaceful overtures from the British Government, on 16 July Adolf Hitler issued his Operational Directive No.16:

◄◄ *Messerschmitt Bf 109s under camouflage netting at a French airfield.*

▼ *A convoy comes under attack off the south coast of England.*

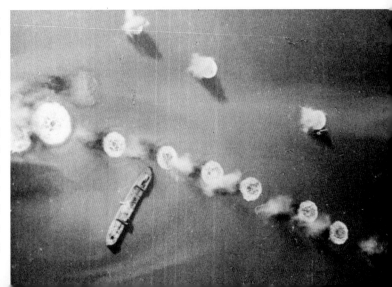

… to eliminate the English homeland as a base for carrying on the war against Germany, and, if it should become necessary, to occupy it completely.

Preparations had to be completed by mid-August, and a series of specific preconditions had to be achieved before an invasion could take place. The first amongst these was:

The English Air Force must have been beaten down to such an extent morally and in actual fact that it can no longer muster any power of attack worth mentioning against the German crossing.

The 19 July was notable for the total eclipse of the Defiant as a day fighter. Although it had achieved some success over

Dunkirk in conjunction with Hurricanes, German pilots soon detected its inherent weakness of relying on guns mounted in a dorsal turret behind the pilot. Nine aircraft of No.141 Squadron were sent on patrol without support. Five were shot down and two others crash-

▲ *A Lysander used for air-sea rescue duties with life-saving gear mounted on the wing stub carrier.*

◀◀ *Four flights of Hurricanes climb in the standard 'Vic' formations.*

33

although No.264 Squadron would make a brief re-appearance in the south in late August.

During this period, RAF pilots came face-to-face with two of the outstanding fighter pilots of the war: Major Adolph Galland of Jagdgeschwader 26 (JG26) and Major Werner Molders of Jagdgeschwader 51 (JG51). Both would rise rapidly to be appointed Kommodore (Wing Commander) of their units.

Shipping off Dover came under constant attack during this early phase and the Royal Navy lost a number of destroyers to bombing raids. On 24 July, No.54 Squadron was heavily involved in defending against concentrated attacks on a convoy near Dover. The Luftwaffe lost fourteen aircraft. Shipping attacks continued the following day, coupled with

▲ *Defiants of No.264 Squadron.*

landed. The two Defiant squadrons were withdrawn and left for the north, where they carried out good work as night fighters,

◀ *Major Werner Molders.*

▼ *Major Adolph Galland, photographed later in the war.*

E-boats trying to penetrate the Royal Navy screens. The 27 July witnessed yet more attacks against Dover. The Royal Navy lost two more destroyers and the port was abandoned as an advanced base for anti-invasion destroyers. This meant that

the defence of the Straits now depended more than ever on the RAF.

Attacks against Dover had become so serious that the Air Ministry issued special instructions to Fighter Command to engage enemy forces approaching the port with superior forces whenever possible. To achieve this concentration in the south-east more squadrons were required and greater use was made of the airfields at Hawkinge and Manston.

For over three weeks the Luftwaffe maintained its attacks against the convoys, which suffered heavy losses – the Admiralty stopped the convoys on 10 August. July had been a month of constant sparring as the Luftwaffe continued to probe Fighter Command's defences. Weaknesses had been exposed, but the robust organisation established by Dowding allowed him and his Group Commanders to rectify them quickly. During this period, Bomber and Coastal Commands had kept up pressure against enemy targets, with the effect of keeping some of the German fighters held back in the occupied countries for defensive duties.

◄ *Pilots of No.17 Squadron at readiness at Martlesham Heath on 20 July 1940.*

▼ *A Spitfire and ground crew of No.609 Squadron at readiness at Middle Wallop.*

➤ *Messerschmitt Bf 110s at low level.*

➤➤ *RAF and Czech pilots of No.310 (Czech) Squadron relax at Duxford.*

➤ *Polish pilots prepare to join the Battle.*

Valuable lessons were learnt during this period. The rigid 'Vic' formation, flown by the fighters of the RAF, were less effective than the Luftwaffe's more flexible and mutually supportive formation, the *Schwarm*, a tactic perfected during the Spanish Civil War. The phase had also clearly highlighted the limitations of the RAF's Defiant fighter. Furthermore, the Luftwaffe had discovered the limitations of the Messerschmitt Bf 110 as an escort fighter, which proved no match for the Hurricanes and Spitfires. This led to the diversion of some of the excellent Messerschmitt Bf 109s to act as a close escort for the large bomber force. Allied to the single-engine fighter's limited range – it could barely reach London – this placed a great restriction on the effectiveness of the fighter, which in turn

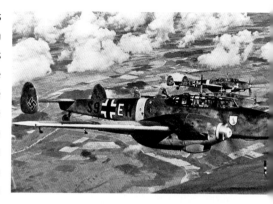

**Did you know?**

The RAF established a listening post at Fairlight in East Sussex, where WAAFs eavesdropped on conversations between German aircrews. Known as the 'Y' Service, much valuable intelligence was gathered.

➤ *Generalleutnant Bruno Loerzer, Commander of two Air Corps – Goering and Galland.*

would have a significant bearing on the battles ahead.

Throughout this phase Dowding had carefully husbanded his resources and there had been a steady build-up of pilots and aircraft. The squadrons in Fighter Command had been bolstered by the availability of Nos 302 and 303 Polish Squadrons and No.310 Czech Squadron, with No.1 (RCAF) Squadron under training. All would join the Battle and perform with distinction.

## SECOND PHASE (8–23 AUGUST)

On 1 August, Hitler issued his Directive No.17, in which he ordered the Luftwaffe to 'use all the forces at its disposal to destroy the British Air Force as quickly as possible.' And so the order for *Adlerangriff*, the 'Attack of the Eagles', was given. This was followed on 8 August by Goering

issuing his order of the day to all units of *Luftflotte* 2, 3 and 5 for Operation *Adler Tag* (Eagle Day) in which they were to 'wipe the British Air Force from the sky'. Within an hour of the order being transmitted, the code breakers at Bletchley had deciphered the signal and it was in the hands of Churchill and Dowding.

40

Many historians, particularly German, consider 8 August as the first day of the Battle of Britain, not without justification. The weight of attack and the bitterness of the fighting was on a new scale. Much of it centred on a convoy, CW 9 – given the code-name 'Peewit', escorted by nine naval vessels. The twenty-ship convoy had sailed from the Thames Estuary the previous evening but the enemy radars on the cliffs at Cap Blanc Nez had detected it. The first morning raid by a force of Ju 87s, escorted by Bf 109s, was broken up, but a second wave at lunchtime managed to break through and scatter the convoy. An even larger attack was mounted late in the afternoon and seven fighter squadrons were scrambled. The scale of the combat exceeded all previous engagements and the Ju 87s suffered heavy losses. Firing the opening shots on this historic day was Squadron Leader J.A.R. Peel, the commanding officer of No.145 Squadron, which he led on all three attacks. The squadron accounted for eleven enemy aircraft and damaged five others. During the day, thirty-one enemy aircraft were shot down for the loss of nineteen RAF fighters.

Early on the morning of 11 August, the Ventnor Radar Station detected a large force of enemy bombers gathering over Cherbourg before it headed towards the Royal Navy base at Portland and the port of Weymouth. Nos 1 and 609 Squadrons were scrambled and others placed at immediate readiness. It was soon realised that the Luftwaffe was mounting a major raid, and by mid-morning eight Hurricane and Spitfire squadrons were engaged in

▼ *A Spitfire of No.152 Squadron, shot down on 8 August. The pilot, Sergeant D.N. Robinson, was injured.*

*A Junkers Ju 88A of 1/KG54, shot down near Portland on 11 August.*

*Blue section of No.609 Squadron scramble from Middle Wallop.*

fierce dogfights with the fighter escort. These allowed many of the Heinkel III and Junkers Ju 88s to bomb from high level and inflict considerable damage on Portland and Weymouth. Losses on both sides were high, with the Luftwaffe losing thirty aircraft and the RAF a similar number.

On 12 August, the Luftwaffe turned its attention to the RAF's fighter airfields and radar stations and the Battle moved forward over the mainland. The Luftwaffe aimed to knock out the early warning radar sites, allowing a stream of bombers to take advantage of the lack of radar coverage to mount heavy attacks against the fighter airfields. The vital Chain Home (CH) Station at Ventnor on the Isle of Wight was one of four RDF stations singled out for attack. Fifteen Junkers Ju 88s of KG51 attacked at noon and were intercepted at 10,000ft – just as they started their attack – by No.152 Squadron Spitfires from Warmwell, as No.609 Squadron took on the fighter escorts. Although the bombers suffered losses they still inflicted heavy

➤ *The remains of a Junkers Ju 88A of 3/KG51, shot down near Portsmouth on 12 August.*

➤➤ *The layout of the Operations Room of a Chain Home station.*

**Did you know?**
The word 'dogfight' was the expression used for a melee of fighter aircraft in combat.

damage, leaving the station off the air and with the majority of buildings destroyed.

The CH stations at Dover, Rye and Pevensey in Kent also suffered damage from bombing, but they were soon back on line, though not before the fighter airfields on the south coast were subjected to heavy raids. Manston, Hawkinge and Lympne were badly damaged but survived. The Luftwaffe fighter escorts stood off during the bombing attacks and tried to entice the British fighters into combat, but RAF pilots had orders to attack the bombers and not be drawn into combat with the escorts.

To plug the gap in the radar coverage that had been provided by the Ventnor station, a mobile radar was moved onto the Isle of Wight and started operating on 23 August until Ventnor was

TYPICAL OPERATIONS ROOM
CHAIN HOME STATION - AUG 1940

**Did you know?**

The last of the RAF's bi-plane fighters, the Gloster Gladiators of No.247 Squadron, flew from Roborough in the defence of the dockyards at Plymouth.

*A Gladiator of No.247 Squadron at Roborough.*

repaired and became operational again in November.

Goering had fixed the date of 13 August for *Adler Tag*, but poor German intelligence and equally poor control and co-ordination of the bomber and fighter forces resulted in confusion and muddle by the attackers and the Luftwaffe suffered heavy losses. No.609 Squadron from Middle Wallop enjoyed particular success. Thirteen of their Spitfires found a formation of Ju 87s with only a small escort and attacked them out of the sun. The dive-bombers scattered and five fell in flames together with two of their escorting Bf 109s. At the end of the day of severe fighting on both flanks of No.11 Group's area, when the Luftwaffe had flown 1,485 sorties – its greatest number to date – thirteen RAF fighters had been lost, but forty-seven German aircraft had been brought down. Goering's Luftwaffe had failed to achieve his boast of knocking out the RAF.

The failure of *Adler Tag* infuriated Goering and on 15 August he summoned his leaders to a conference when he reiterated the need for the Ju 87s to be given a strong fighter escort, which must remain with them. In the meantime, in France, the largest German force so far assembled was ready for take-off, and it was to be the Luftwaffe's greatest effort during the Battle. The target for the German airmen was Fighter Command itself. It aimed to attack the ground organisation and draw the fighters into the air where they would be destroyed. A new dimension was added with a synchronised attack by aircraft of *Luftflotte* 5 – based in Norway

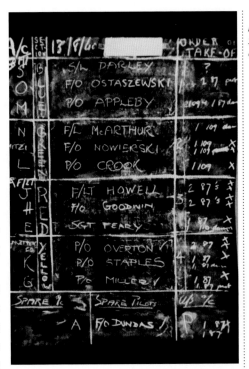

◀ *The operation's board of No.609 Squadron, showing the claims of 13 August.*

**Did you know?**
Fifty-three Fleet Air Arm pilots flew with Fighter Command during the Battle.

➤ *The Daily Express reported the big events of 12 August.*

**Daily Express**

No. 12,556                    Tuesday, August 13, 1940                    One Penny

## The Battle of Britain is on: Hitler throws in more and more bombers

# BIGGEST AIR RAIDS OF ALL

*R.A.F. shoots down 39 more Nazis and loses only nine fighters*

He gave his life to save town..

'Britain's new terrifying weapon'

## ALBANIANS KILL 400 ITALIANS

Belgrade report

### PORTSMOUTH HEAVILY BOMBED

*Daily Express Air Reporter BASIL CARDEW*

HITLER intensified his mass air raids on British ports still further yesterday. Even more aircraft than he used in the mass attacks on Thursday and Sunday were sent against Portsmouth and the Kent coast.

**Afterthoughts on raiding Britain by**

# FIVE CAPTURED RAIDERS

*Here are stories sent from five south-east coast towns last night.*

**THE REALIST**

A BADLY wounded German airman came down by parachute in a field. A farm groom covered him with a shotgun. The airman flung up his hands.

And then he said : "No more fighting. English too good."

Former A.R.P. chief held

## STOP PRESS

**MOUNTAIN GRAVE FOR SIR ABE BAILEY**

**FRICK TO INSPECT OCCUPIED FRANCE**

**B.B.C. FADES OUT**

U.S. mission 'a step towards war'

Three little girls buried alive

*DOCTOR OPERATED AS BOMBS BURST*

*Daily Express Staff Reporter BERNARD HALL*

162 seavacuees arrive

Mr. Coward has plans for "after the war"

and Denmark – against the airfields in the north-east of Britain, with the aim of drawing Dowding's reserves from the south.

The squadrons in Nos 12 and 13 Groups were forewarned, and the lunchtime attack was repelled with heavy losses. Further south, large formations of bombers attacked the airfields but poor German intelligence had failed to identify the key sector airfields, resulting in less important ones bearing the brunt of the attacks. Throughout the day the Luftwaffe had flown 1,786 sorties for the loss of at least seventy-six aircraft, a day that they would remember as 'Black Thursday'.

The following day the raids in the south continued with unabated fury. At lunchtime a large force of Ju 87s headed straight for Tangmere. Three Hurricane squadrons, Nos 1, 43 and 601, waded into them, but the sector airfield suffered

◄ *Flight Lieutenant Archie McKellar of No.605 Squadron intercepted Heinkel He IIIs near Newcastle. He shot at least one down and was awarded the DFC. He was killed in October 1940.*

49

➤ *Spitfires of No.616 Squadron at readiness at Leconfield on 15 August.*

**Did you know?**

The name 'Hellfire Corner' was given to the area around Folkestone and Dover, where so much fighting in the air and at sea took place.

major damage with many fires breaking out and buildings destroyed. The station's medical services distinguished themselves, and for his gallantry under fire the senior medical officer, Flight Lieutenant Courtney Willey, was awarded the Military Cross.

Although seven of the dive-bombers had been destroyed, every hangar had been hit together with workshops, sick been hit together with workshops, sick quarters and the Officers' Mess. Twenty personnel had been killed and many more injured.

◄ *Junkers Ju 87s at low level.*

➤ *Airmen also paid the ultimate sacrifice when Tangmere was attacked on 16 August.*

Later in the afternoon, Flight Lieutenant James Nicolson – a flight commander with No.249 Squadron – earned Fighter Command's sole Victoria Cross. He remained at the controls of his blazing Hurricane to continue an attack on an enemy fighter, which he shot down before bailing out, wounded and badly burned. As he descended by parachute, a group of soldiers opened fire on him and he received further wounds.

The Luftwaffe's all-out efforts to destroy Fighter Command in one week ended with a major assault on 18 August, a day dubbed by some as 'The Hardest Day,' which saw the fiercest fighting of the Battle, when both the RAF and the Luftwaffe suffered some of the heaviest losses. During the course of the day the Luftwaffe launched three major attacks,

*◄◄ The Victoria Cross.*

*◄ Flight Lieutenant James Nicolson, Fighter Command's only Victoria Cross holder.*

**Did you know?**

The name given to
the life jackets worn
by aircrew was *Mae
West,* after the well-
endowed American
film actress.

primarily against airfields in southern England. A co-ordinated attack from high and low level caused serious damage at Kenley, but a similar attack against Biggin Hill was less successful. Croydon was hit later in the day and suffered extensive damage, but each of the sector airfields continued to operate their squadrons. During the afternoon, the Hurricanes of No.43 Squadron intercepted a force of Ju 87 dive-bombers just as they were about to commence an attack against the radar at Poling near Chichester. Five were shot down within minutes, before fighters from Nos 152, 601 and 602 appeared on the scene to complete the massacre. In all, the British fighters accounted for sixteen Ju 87s, and this particular day signalled the virtual demise of the dive-bomber, which had

suffered very heavy losses over the previous weeks.

Over the next few days the weather intervened and allowed Fighter Command some respite and a chance to replace aircraft and pilots, although the availability of pilots was always Dowding's greatest concern. The increased production of fighters and the miracles performed by the ground crews on the airfields ensured that sufficient numbers would be available.

On 20 August, Churchill rose in the House of Commons to pay his unforgettable tribute to Fighter Command which immortalised the handful of Allied pilots, concluding his speech with:

Never in the field of human conflict was so much owed by so many to so few.

*A Dornier Do 17 plunges to earth.*

◄◄ *A Dornier Do 17Z-2 of 9/KG76, brought down near Leaves Green, near Biggin Hill, on 18 August.*

◄ *Flight Sergeant 'Grumpy' Unwin of No.19 Squadron, one of the RAF's most successful pilots, with his dog Flash.*

*Pilots of No.19 Squadron rush to their Spitfires at Duxford.*

### Did you know?

In addition to Great Britain, the men who flew with the RAF in the Battle came from fourteen other countries.

*Polish pilots on standby.*

## THIRD PHASE (24 AUGUST– 6 SEPTEMBER)

Regarded as the crucial phase of the Battle, the Luftwaffe endeavoured to force the RAF to abandon its airfields in the south-east and heavy raids were mounted against Hornchurch and Manston, the latter having to be temporarily abandoned.

There were two significant developments on 24 August which had a major bearing on the conduct of the rest of the Battle. With all his squadrons airborne to meet large-scale attacks, Park called on Air Vice-Marshal Trafford Leigh-Mallory's squadrons of No.12 Group to protect his airfields to the north of the Thames. Leigh-Mallory was fresh to fighter operations and had been heavily influenced by one of his squadron commanders, Squadron Leader Douglas Bader, who was impatient

*➤ Three 'Vics' of Hurricanes climb.*

to engage the enemy. He claimed that three squadrons formed into a 'Big Wing' would be more effective than individual squadrons. However, forming such a large formation took time, and, apart from No.19 Squadron, Leigh-Mallory's other squadrons arrived too late to prevent serious damage at North Weald, Debden and Hornchurch. The 'Big Wing' controversy would be a bone of contention for the rest of the Battle and long after.

The other major event of this day was an attack at night by a force of 100 bombers, and for the first time since 1918 bombs fell on London, albeit their primary target being the Thames Haven oil storage depot. Goering was furious that Hitler's orders had been 'disobeyed'. However, within twenty-four hours it precipitated an immediate retaliatory attack by eighty-one

RAF bombers against Berlin, an action that would contribute to a chain of events that would swing the Battle in favour of Fighter Command.

Heavy raids were mounted on 26 August when airfields in the south-east and others north of the Thames came under heavy attack. The Luftwaffe suffered heavy losses, but Fighter Command suffered badly too with the loss of twenty-six aircraft, four from the recently arrived No.616 Squadron. Park was very concerned that No.12 Group fighters had once again failed to protect his airfields north of the Thames, and he drew a stark comparison with the routine and timely support he received from No.10 Group to the west of his area. Night raids against industrial centres began. Intense fighting continued, and despite inflicting heavy losses against

► *The crew of No.51 Squadron Whitley prepare to take-off from Dishforth.*

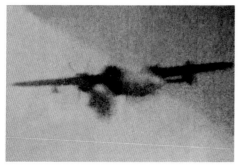

the Luftwaffe, the loss of RAF pilots was mounting.

Goering too had problems. He became increasingly impatient with his fighter pilots, yet failed to appreciate that it was his order – that the capable Bf 109s must stick to the bombers – that greatly restricted their freedom of action. This inflexibility, allied to the Bf 109s limited fuel for air combat, caused great frustration amongst the Luftwaffe's fighter leaders. To provide greater support for his bombers, Goering transferred the fighters of *Luftflotte 3* to reinforce the squadrons in the Pas de Calais. Stripped of its fighters, *Luftflotte 3* was forced to concentrate on the night bombing campaign.

Airfields in the south continued to come under heavy attack on 28 August. A mixed group of Dornier 17s and Heinkel IIIs appeared early in the morning, with a strong escort of Bf 109s, heading towards Rochford and Eastchurch. The ill-fated Defiants of No.264 Squadron tried to intercept but four were shot down. Eastchurch was badly damaged, but it was a Coastal Command airfield and Luftwaffe intelligence had once again proved lacking. Darkness signalled a series of attacks against the cities, with over 100 bombers heading for Liverpool and

*Messerschmitt Bf 109s of 9/JG 2 take-off.*

**Did you know?**
'Scramble' was the word used to order take-off immediately. It was often accompanied with the ringing of a bell or a fire warning triangle.

causing widespread damage. This was to be the first of four consecutive night raids on Liverpool.

Heavy raids against the airfields continued on 30 August, when Biggin Hill

▼ *Squadron Leader Peter Townsend, OC 85 Squadron, with his ground crew.*

suffered severe damage from a surprise low-level attack by nine Junker 88s. An air-raid shelter was hit and the death toll was thirty-nine, including many members of the WAAF. The Observer Corps on the South Coast also reported a heavy raid heading for the Thames, and the Hurricanes of Squadron Leader Peter Townsend's No.85 Squadron put in a withering head-on attack and split the formation up. The fighting on this day had been the heaviest experienced by Dowding's pilots so far, who had flown 1,054 sorties.

The following day saw Fighter Command's biggest losses as the Luftwaffe mounted large raids against the fighter airfields, but it was Biggin Hill that once again suffered the most damage. Fighter Command lost thirty-seven aircraft, most of them in fighter-to-fighter combat. The

◄ *Gunners of the 90th Anti-Aircraft Regiment at Biggin Hill.*

**Did you know?**
At the end of July, 1,466 balloons had been allocated to the various squadrons of Balloon Command.

**Did you know?**

'Tally-ho!', an expression used in hunting to announce that the hounds had seen a fox, was used by the leader of a fighter formation to indicate that he had sighted the enemy.

exploits of pilots has always been well recorded, but the operations of that day also highlighted the outstanding efforts of those on the ground who worked under intense pressure and danger and undertook many acts of gallantry. Two WAAFs manning the crucial telephone exchange, Sergeant Helen Turner – a WRAF veteran of the First World War – and Corporal Elspeth Henderson, remained at their posts in the operations block as bombs once again rained down on Biggin Hill. They were subsequently awarded the Military Medal for their bravery.

The beginning of September saw attacks against the sector airfields continue, and Biggin Hill experienced its sixth raid in three days. It also saw a more determined effort by the Luftwaffe to attack aircraft factories, which were working overtime to replace aircraft losses. Park tasked some of his squadrons to provide cover to the Hawker and Vickers Supermarine factories in the south. Almost immediately these tactics paid off. When enemy bombers tried to get through to Brooklands – where half of the Hurricanes were built – the squadrons on patrol prevented any serious damage. Early September also saw a major escalation in the night bombing of towns and cities, but there were few squadrons available to attack the raiders.

There was to be no respite for Fighter Command, and pilots were sometimes scrambled four or five times a day. The intense and remorseless fighting by day continued, and losses mounted with the availability of pilots once again causing Dowding much concern. His forces were suffering from accumulated fatigue and

◄ *Biggin Hill's three WAAF Military Medallists, Sergeant Elizabeth Mortimer, Corporal (later commissioned) Elspeth Henderson and Sergeant Helen Turner.*

*◄◄ A Messerschmitt Bf 109E of II/JG3, forced down near Marden, Kent, on 5 September.*

*◄ Pilots of No.19 Squadron scramble in their Spitfires.*

71

| YEAR 1940 | | AIRCRAFT | | PILOT, OR 1ST PILOT | 2ND PILOT, PUPIL OR PASSENGER | DUTY (INCLUDING RESULTS AND REMARKS) |
|---|---|---|---|---|---|---|
| MONTH | DATE | Type | No. | | | |
| — | — | — | — | — | — | TOTALS BROUGHT FORWARD |
| Aug | 29 | SPITFIRE | X.4184 | SELF | | X RAID. |
| " | " | " | " | " | | X RAID. |
| " | 30 | " | " | " | | X RAID. |
| " | " | " | " | " | | X RAID. |
| " | " | " | " | " | | INTERCEPTED: He.III & Me.110. (1 He.III Prob. 1 He.III Damaged) |
| " | " | " | " | " | | X RAID. |
| " | " | " | " | " | | X RAID. |
| " | 31 | " | " | " | | X RAID. |
| " | " | " | " | " | | X RAID. |

SUMMARY FOR AUGUST. 1940.      TYPES.

No. 615 Sqn.   R.A.F.
No. 616 Sqn.   R.A.F.      { HURRICANE SPITFIRE MAGISTER.

L. d'Arcy      5/9/40.

O.C. No 616 Sqn. U.B...

GRAND TOTAL [Cols. (1) to (10)]   85 Hrs. 10 Mins.   TOTALS CARRIED FORWARD

he had lost 300 pilots, many of whom were his most experienced, yet only 270 arrived to replace them, the great majority only recently out of training and with little or no experience in air fighting. Dowding had rotated his squadrons and allowed the exhausted ones to move north to reorganise and re-equip, but by September 7 Fighter Command was approaching a crisis. The situation on the No.11 Group sector airfields was becoming critical, with four so badly damaged that they were becoming unusable. With other airfields in the Group damaged there became a distinct possibility that squadrons might have to have been withdrawn to more distant airfields.

During the previous two weeks 295 fighters had been lost and a further 171 seriously damaged. The aircraft factories

◄◄ *A page from the log book of Pilot Officer 'Buck' Casson of No.616 Squadron, which illustrates the intensity of the battle.*

◄ *Invasion barges at Dunkirk.*

➤➤ *Men of the Observer Corps at their post at Blunsdon.*

**Did you know?**

During the war, the ringing of church bells was forbidden, being reserved as the signal of a coming invasion.

had improved production but were struggling to keep up with the rate of attrition.

Throughout this critical period, the RAF's photographic reconnaissance aircraft had kept a constant watch on the Channel ports and brought back evidence that many invasion barges were being concentrated at the French and Belgian Channel ports. The Air Ministry issued to Commands its Invasion Alert No.1 (Attack Imminent), and Bomber Command intensified its attacks against the barges.

## FOURTH PHASE (7–30 SEPTEMBER)

Just as Dowding's problems mounted, Goering made the astonishing decision to abandon his attacks against the airfields and switch his bombers to attack London. He travelled in his extravagantly furnished train and moved to Pas de Calais to take personal command of the air assault. The morning of 7 September was unusually quiet and there was little activity for six hours. Then, in mid-afternoon came an Observer Corps report that 'many hundreds' of aircraft were approaching the coast near Dover. By 4.30p.m. Park had ordered into the air all twenty-one squadrons based within seventy miles of London. As they climbed they were confronted by an awesome wall of bombers and they plunged into the attack.

Almost 1,000 bombers, along with a heavy fighter escort, had been dispatched to undertake an all-out attack against London. Bombs rained down on the docks and fires raged, which served only to provide a beacon for the night bombers. War had come to the civilian population

and casualties were high. They were to endure many nights of bombing and resulting destruction.

On 9 September, Goering ordered the 'round-the-clock' bombing of London using Kesselring's bombers, escorted by fighters, and Sperrle's *Luftflotte* 3 unescorted bombers by night. In the meantime, and in spite of Goering's abandonment of the destruction of the RAF in favour of destroying the will of the people of London, Hitler pressed on with his intention of launching Operation Sealion. He decided to issue the warning order for the invasion on 14 September, with the intention of mounting it ten days later – assuming that Goering had gained air superiority. It is not clear how he expected this would be achieved following the Luftwaffe's diversion to the attacks against London.

◀◀ *Dornier Do 17s head across the English Channel.*

◀ *A ship-mounted balloon in the River Thames.*

➤ *Post Office engineers repair cables in a bomb crater.*

The scrappy fighting and the few losses they had sustained over the previous few days led the Luftwaffe generals to believe that Fighter Command was beginning to collapse, a view that was conveyed to Goering and on to Hitler. In fact, Park had merely changed his tactics. In order to meet the Luftwaffe in maximum strength he established a different readiness system and ordered his squadrons to attack in a series of pairs, with the Spitfires to take on the Bf 109s and the Hurricanes to attack the bombers and their close escorts. Night attacks against London continued and the anti-aircraft defences were strengthened. Night raids were also mounted against Southampton and Portsmouth.

Hitler gathered his commanders in Berlin on 13 September. He praised the Luftwaffe for their efforts but again acknowledged

◄ *Spitfires of No.19 Squadron attack a formation of Heinkel He III bombers.*

Keith Woodcock

**Did you know?**
The classification of invasion warnings was: Alert 3 – 'Invasion probable within three days'; Alert 2 – '… within two days'; and Alert 1 – '…imminent'.

➤➤ *A Hurricane of No.601 Squadron in its blast pen at Tangmere.*

➤➤ *Ground crew descend on a No.609 Squadron for a rapid turnaround.*

that for a successful invasion 'complete air superiority is required'. He blamed the recent weather for failure to achieve this, but clearly he had, once again, been fed over-optimistic intelligence. Despite losing eighty barges as a result of RAF bombing, as well as the reserves of the navy, Hitler decided to continue with his invasion plans and postponed Sealion again.

The date of 15 September will always be synonymous with the Battle, and indeed it has been celebrated as the 'Battle of Britain Day' ever since. The Germans had planned another major raid against London, and the Fighter Command radar screens showed massed formations building up over Calais and Boulogne late in the morning. This gave Park time to position the fighters of both Nos 11 and 12 Groups. The Hurricanes attacked the huge formation of bombers as it approached the south coast as the Spitfires engaged the fighter escort. More RAF squadrons were scrambled and directed to the enemy formation and a huge air battle followed. As the enemy fighters used their fuel in combat and were forced to return, the enemy bombers were left unprotected as they approached London where the Duxford Wing fell on them. The bombers scattered and unloaded their bombs at random before turning back for France, harried all the way by Hurricanes and Spitfires.

By coincidence, Winston Churchill made a visit to No.11 Group's Operations Room at Uxbridge and witnessed the battle unfold. At its height, he asked Air Vice-Marshal Park if there were any reserves left, to which Park made his famous reply, 'There are none.'

At the end of the day, the BBC announced '185 shot down', a huge boost for the morale of the public – in the event, the German losses were actually much less. The German High Command had expected great things of the Luftwaffe on that day. After the apparently successful efforts of the previous days, Goering had convinced himself – and hence also others – that the RAF was about to collapse. Instead the losses incurred were higher than any

▼ *Hurricanes of No.85 Squadron scramble.*

➤ *A Heinkel He III is lifted from the sea.*

**Did you know?**
The Luftwaffe always considered the Battle of Britain to have commenced on 10 August 1940. Deployed against Great Britain were 3,358 aircraft, of which 2,550 were serviceable.

day since 18 August. These heavy losses caused major recriminations amongst the German bomber crews, who complained of the incessant RAF attacks by squadrons that supposedly did not exist according to German intelligence and propaganda.

The Luftwaffe returned to night attacks against London and other cities but, Bomber and Coastal Command aircraft were also out in force daily, inflicting heavy damage on the growing fleet of barges gathering at the French and Belgian ports. In addition, secret intelligence intercepted German signals instructing the staff on Dutch airfields to dismantle the air-loading equipment for the troop-carrying transport aircraft. Hitler had once again postponed Operation Sealion, this time indefinitely.

In the last two weeks of September the weather deteriorated and the Luftwaffe changed its tactics. Goering sent his bombers against the aircraft factories, and the Bristol facility at Filton suffered heavy damage when Heinkel IIIs attacked on 25 September. The following day the Supermarine factory at Southampton was hit. Although there was heavy damage and casualties, the creation of 'shadow factories' in the Midlands were able to maintain a steady production line.

Night attacks against British cities continued and there were more daylight encounters with bomber forces, though these became infrequent. However, on 27 September *Luftflotte* 2 made renewed attempts to bomb London in daylight and a large formation was broken up by Park's squadrons. A failure of co-ordination left the Junker Ju 88s without an adequate fighter escort and the Spitfires and

**Did you know?**
Ten citizens of the United States served in Fighter Command during the Battle of Britain. Pilot Officer 'Billy' Fiske, of No.601 Squadron, crash-landed at Tangmere on 16 August after a combat with Junker Ju 87 aircraft. He died the following day and there is a memorial to him in St Paul's Cathedral.

◀◀ *Bombing up a Blenheim IV of No.110 Squadron at Wattisham, prior to attacking the German's invasion fleet of barges.*

◀ *Pilots of No.504 Squadron rest at Filton in September 1940.*

Hurricanes fell on the bombers. Eventually the Bf 109s appeared on the scene, but not before at least fifteen bombers and six Bf 110s had been shot down. A later raid by *Luftflotte* 3 broke into two, with a large section heading for London and

another for Bristol. Both were intercepted and suffered heavy losses. By the end of the day, the RAF had lost twenty-eight fighters but the Luftwaffe had lost fifty-four. Churchill declared, '27 September ranks as the third great and victorious day of Fighter Command during the course of the Battle of Britain.'

On 30 September, the Luftwaffe launched a series of strong attacks, trying to reach

<< A 4.5 anti-aircraft site in the west of England.

<< Anti-aircraft fire over London.

< The historic Church of St Mary le Bow, burnt out after raids in the east of London.

*Oberleutenant Karl Fisher of 7/JG27 force-landed his damaged Messerschmitt Bf 109E in Windsor Great Park.*

them being Bf 109s. The Poles of No.303 Squadron were amongst the most successful.

## FIFTH PHASE (1–31 OCTOBER)

Bomber Command continued their almost nightly attacks against the Channel ports harbouring the invasion barges. After the heavy losses during the final days of September, the Luftwaffe commanders decided that all twin-engine bombers should be withdrawn from daylight attacks and used almost exclusively at night. Fighter sweeps were introduced, with Bf 110s in the bomber role escorted by Bf 109s – some of these carrying a single bomb – conducting 'hit and run' raids which proved particularly difficult to counter, but these tactics were never likely to be decisive.

London and the Westland aircraft factory at Yeovil. The majority were repulsed and the Luftwaffe retreated with heavy losses, with at least forty-two shot down, thirty of

By early October Fighter Command had rebuilt some of its strength and

was reaching full establishment, but its night-fighter force was still very weak, although the Beaufighter was beginning to appear on the scene. The two Defiant squadrons in the north had some success, but the airborne interception radars in

the Blenheim squadrons proved to be inadequate.

Raids throughout October continued, but they were widespread and on a small scale. It was on 8 October that the Czech, Sergeant Josef Frantisek DFM, died. His seventeen confirmed victories, all achieved in the crucial thirty days of September, made him the RAF's top-scoring pilot of the Battle of Britain. On 12 October, Operation Sealion was postponed till the spring of 1941, and on 29 October the Luftwaffe carried out its last large daylight raid when it was forced to retreat having incurred heavy losses. The pilots of No.602 Squadron distinguished themselves by shooting down eight Messerschmitts in ten minutes. The last 'official' day of the Battle turned out to be the quietest for four months. Not a single aircraft of either air force was lost in combat.

Without air supremacy over southern England, no German invasion could be successfully attempted. Goering's Luftwaffe had proved incapable of delivering his boast that the RAF's fighter forces would be annihilated 'within two or three days'. After the war, the outstanding

◄◄ *The crew of No.29 Squadron man their Blenheim 1F Night Fighter.*

▼ *Flight Lieutenant F. Howell and Pilot Officer S.J. Hill, with their trophy from a Junkers Ju 88 they shot down to record No.609 Squadron's 100th kill.*

Some of 'The Few' – pilots of No.610 Squadron at Hawkinge.

No.1 Squadron's Standard with the battle honour, 'Battle of Britain', emblazoned.

**Did you know?**
No.1 (RCAF) Squadron was the only Commonwealth squadron to participate in the Battle. It flew Hurricanes from Middle Wallop and Northolt. In 1941 it was re-numbered No.401 Squadron.

German fighter leader, Adolph Galland, commented:

From the first the British had an extraordinary advantage, never to be balanced out at any time during the war, which was their radar and fighter control network and organisation. It was for us a very bitter surprise. We had nothing like it. We could do no other than knock frontally against the outstandingly well organised and resolute direct defence of the British Isles.

A fitting tribute to Dowding, to his air defence system and to his 'dear fighter boys' – The Few.

Battle of Britain Day is commemorated in the United Kingdom on 15 September. During the nearest weekend the RAF mount a flypast over London, and on the Sunday a Thanksgiving Service is held in Westminster Abbey. For many years, RAF Stations opened their gates to the general public for their annual 'At Home' day, but in more recent years large air shows have been held at selected major RAF stations.

The major anniversaries have been commemorated with a series of events. Members of the Battle of Britain Fighter Association, eligible only if one was part of the aircrew of Fighter Command who flew during the Battle, were entertained in 1960 by Her Majesty's Government at Lancaster House and by the City of London at Guildhall in 1965, 1980 and 1990. To celebrate the 50th Anniversary in

2966

**Battle of Britain Week**

**ROYAL AIR FORCE at home BINBROOK** *Jet Bomber Station*

SATURDAY, 14th SEPTEMBER, 1957

**SOUVENIR PROGRAMME - ONE SHILLING**

◄ *RAF Binbrook's 'At Home' day in 1957.*

1990, veterans were invited to Buckingham Palace, and on the following day a major parade was held in front of Buckingham

**Did you know?**
On 13 September 1940, bombs fell on the centre of London, when Buckingham Palace was hit for the third time and the Royal Chapel was wrecked.

Palace in the presence of Her Majesty the Queen. Seventeen RAF Standards of serving Battle of Britain squadrons were on parade together, with others representing the Royal Australian Air Force, the Royal Canadian Air Force, the Royal New Zealand Air Force, the Royal Auxiliary Air Force, the Royal Observer Corps and numerous veterans' associations. A flypast of seven separate formations, which included 160 aircraft, flew over the parade.

For many years, members of the Battle of Britain Fighter Association were concerned that there was no statue in London to commemorate their wartime chief during the Battle, then Air Chief Marshal Sir Hugh Dowding. After overcoming many difficulties, and thanks to generous donations, a splendidly sculpted bronze statue was erected outside the Royal Air Force church, St Clement Danes in the Strand. It was unveiled by Her Majesty the Queen Mother on 30 October 1988.

## BATTLE OF BRITAIN MEMORIAL FLIGHT

In the years immediately following the Second World War it became traditional for a Hurricane and a Spitfire to lead the annual commemorative Victory Day flypast over London. With the advent of the jet age these aircraft, once the mainstay of RAF fighter operations, were withdrawn from service. By the mid-1950s there was only one airworthy Hurricane in the RAF, based at RAF Biggin Hill. With the phasing out of service of the Spitfire in 1957 there was a strong belief among some in the RAF that the service's greatest Battle Honour should continue to be commemorated in a fitting fashion – and the best way to do

*◀ Air and ground crew veterans of No.616 Squadron at the 50th Anniversary celebrations at Buckingham Palace.*

➤➤ *Battle of Britain Flight's Spitfire and Hurricane at Kemble, September 2009.*

**Did you know?**

Towards the end of the Battle, the Luftwaffe's outstanding single-seat Messerschmitt Bf 109E fighter was modified to carry bombs.

that was to keep these legendary fighters in the air.

Due to the enthusiasm and foresight of Wing Commander Peter Thompson DFC, himself a Battle of Britain pilot, the Historic Aircraft Flight was formed at Biggin Hill, where Thompson was the Station Commander. He gained the authority to form the unit, but there would be no public funding and all manpower would have to be voluntary. From these somewhat humble beginnings, the Flight developed over the years on a more formal footing, and in April 1963 it moved to RAF Coltishall when it was established with a team of full-time engineers.

After filming for the 1969 cinema classic *Battle of Britain*, the Flight was presented with Spitfire IIa P7350. This was (and still is) the world's oldest airworthy example of its type, and a genuine combat veteran of the Battle of Britain. Having popularly become known as the Battle of Britain Memorial Flight (BBMF), it took this name officially on 1 June 1969.

On 20 November 1973 a new and significant type arrived, Lancaster I PA474, transferred from RAF Waddington where it had been refurbished and looked after by station personnel. It had been making a growing number of appearances and station resources were struggling to keep pace with the demand. It was decided to place the Lancaster under the care of the BBMF, which had the necessary expertise to maintain it.

Less than two years later, it was announced that the BBMF was moving to RAF Coningsby in Lincolnshire, where it became established on 1 March 1976

➤ *The Battle of Britain Flight.*

**Did you know?**

The oldest flying participant in the Battle was Pilot Officer Sydney Carling, an air gunner with No.264 Squadron, who at the age of 51 already held the MC, DFC and DCM. He had lost a leg in the First World War and shot down eleven aircraft. He was killed in May 1941.

and where its hangar and a visitor centre is open to the public.

Since its inception in 1957, the aircrews on the Flight have been drawn from volunteers, all of whom perform a primary duty flying a variety of aircraft in the RAF inventory. The one exception is the Officer Commanding, who oversees operations, administration and engineering.

In the early period, the Flight was tasked with between 50 to 60 appearances a year. From these small beginnings the tasking has increased significantly. In 2009 the BBMF were tasked with over 900 individual appearances at more than 500 separate events. These included 127 air displays and 402 flypasts of various sizes, ranging from the Queen's Birthday Flypast over London, through commemorative flypasts for veterans such as the 65th Anniversary of D-Day and Arnhem and the 60th Anniversary of the Berlin Airlift, to small village fêtes.

Today, in addition to the Lancaster, the Flight has five Spitfires, two Hurricanes and a Dakota, all of which appear regularly on the air show circuit. It also operates the RAF's last two Chipmunks which are used for training the fighter pilots on tailwheel aircraft.

## NATIONAL MEMORIAL TO THE FEW – CAPEL-LE-FERNE

Many years after the Battle of Britain, one of the veterans of the Battle, Wing Commander Geoffrey Page DSO, DFC and Bar, realised to his astonishment that there was no national memorial to his comrades who had fought in the summer of 1940. As a twenty year old, Geoffrey Page had fought with No.56 Squadron, being shot

**Did you know?**
An element of the Italian *Regia Aeronautica*, called the Italian Air Corps (*Corpo Aereo Italiano* or CAI), took part in the latter stages of the Battle. It first saw action in late October 1940 but it achieved very limited success.

➤➤ *The memorial at Capel-le-Ferne.*

**Did you know?**
The highest-scoring pilot during the Battle, with a total of seventeen victories, was Czech-born Sergeant Josef Frantisek of No.303 (Polish) Squadron. He was killed on 8 October 1940.

down into the sea and very badly burned. He became a 'Guinea Pig', one of those treated by the plastic surgery team of Archie McIndoe. In due course, he returned to action.

To provide a lasting memorial to his colleagues of Fighter Command who had fought in the Battle he founded the Battle of Britain Memorial Trust, and it was his drive and determination that established the poignant memorial at Capel-le-Ferne on the cliffs of Kent, in the area that was known as 'Hellfire Corner' in 1940. On 9 July 1993, Her Majesty the Queen Mother came to Capel-le-Ferne and unveiled the memorial. In the middle of a three-bladed propeller a young airman sits looking contemplatively out to the Straits of Dover.

The original concept for the memorial was to include a wall on which all the names of 'The Few' would appear. Principally through the benefaction of the late Air Chief Marshal Sir Christopher Foxley-Norris, GCB, DSO, OBE, a Hurricane pilot with No.3 Squadron, a Memorial Wall was added to the site in 2005 when HRH Prince Michael of Kent, the Patron of the Battle of Britain Memorial Trust, officiated at its launch. This wall of fifteen panels contains the names of almost 3,000 Allied aircrew who flew in the Battle.

The RAF's two principal fighter aircraft of the time are represented at the memorial with replicas of a Hurricane of No.56 Squadron and a Spitfire of No.65 Squadron. A visitor centre, the Hunting Lodge, has recently been expanded. Display boards nearby are dedicated to the memory of Pilot Officer Herbert Case of No.72 Squadron, whose Spitfire crashed near the memorial site on 12 October 1940.

The Battle of Britain Memorial Trust maintains the memorial site and relies almost entirely on voluntary support and private donations. In 2000, The Friends of The Few was established to support the work of the Memorial Trust and welcomes new members.

▼ *Veterans Bob Foster, Pete Brothers and Bam Bamberger at the 2004 Memorial Day at Capel-le-Ferne.*

➤➤ *Air Chief Marshal Lord Dowding laid the foundation stone of Biggin Hill's St George's Chapel on 25 July 1951.*

**Did you know?**

'The Few' were 2,353 young men from Great Britain and 574 from overseas – pilots and other aircrew – who are officially recognised as having taken part in the Battle of Britain.

## ST GEORGE'S ROYAL AIR FORCE CHAPEL OF REMEMBRANCE – BIGGIN HILL

The idea to create a permanent chapel at RAF Biggin Hill emerged in 1943 to remember those aircrew who had been killed on operations from within the Biggin Hill sector, especially those who had died in the Battle of Britain. Three prefabricated huts, made with steel angle-iron frames and lined with fibreboard, were acquired and placed together to form a single rectangular unit as a chapel. A commemorative service, unveiling and dedicating the memorial – the reredos – and the Book of Remembrance, was held on Battle of Britain Sunday, 19 September 1943.

St George's Chapel was loved by many who served at Biggin Hill during the latter stages of the war, and equally well loved by Winston Churchill, whose home at Chartwell was some seven miles south of Biggin Hill.

The chapel survived the remainder of the war, but one night in December 1946 it caught fire and was almost totally destroyed. When Winston Churchill heard of this destruction, he was extremely distressed. He felt strongly that a permanent memorial chapel should be built and funds were raised through a national appeal. The design chosen was based on the original chapel and was intended to recapture the austerity, simplicity and atmosphere, as well as the size and shape of the wartime huts.

The foundation stone was laid by Air Chief Lord Dowding in July 1951, and the building was dedicated by the Bishop of Rochester in November of that year.

The main body of the chapel is beautifully decorated with twelve stained-

▲ The reredos in
St George's Chapel
records the names of the
pilots killed flying from
the Biggin Hill Sector.

In the Sanctuary there are six panels of the reredos either side of the altar. On these panels are recorded the names of 453 aircrew who lost their lives on operations from the Biggin Hill sector. The main campaigns are recorded across the top. Flags of the Commonwealth and Allied countries of airmen who served at Biggin Hill flank the altar. The Book of Remembrance is contained in a glass-topped display cabinet, and the page on view is turned each day to correspond to the actual day showing.

There are five windows in St George's Room. The main window illustrates the symbolic victory of St George over the forces of evil, shown as the Luftwaffe. The remaining four windows, installed in 1986, commemorate the various ground services which were essential to keep the station

glass windows of exceptional quality. They are of matching design and show a young man with six wings holding in front of his chest the badges of squadrons that served at Biggin Hill during the Battle of Britain, of other higher RAF formations and of the Hurricane and Spitfire.

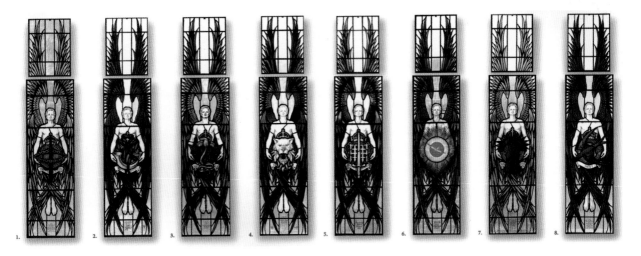

1.    2.    3.    4.    5.    6.    7.    8.

operational but which were until then not recognised in the chapel.

The gates of the chapel are flanked by a replica Hurricane, representing No.79 Squadron, and a Spitfire representing No.92 Squadron. The Garden of Remembrance was consecrated by the RAF's Chaplain-in-Chief, the Venerable Brian Lucas, on 22 June 1995.

The chapel, which is an active church, is open daily to visitors and is supported by the Friends of St George's Chapel.

▲ *The stained-glass windows in St George's Chapel.*

## BATTLE OF BRITAIN MEMORIAL – EMBANKMENT, LONDON

On 18 September 2005, to commemorate the 65th Anniversary of the Battle of Britain, HRH Prince Charles dedicated the Battle of Britain Memorial on Victoria Embankment, London.

The memorial, commissioned by the Battle of Britain Historical Society, is made up of two bronze friezes set in an 82ft granite structure. A walkway has been cut obliquely through the middle of the structure. The bronze reliefs, by the sculptor Paul Day, depict aspects of the achievements of Fighter Command in the air and of the ground crew, while the other focuses on the people of London, featuring St Paul's Cathedral and an Anderson air-raid shelter. The central feature of the relief facing the road represents pilots scrambling

**Did you know?**

Shortly after the end of the Battle, Air Chief Marshal Sir Hugh Dowding and Air Vice-Marshal Keith Park, the two architects of the victory, were replaced as Commander-in-Chief of Fighter Command and AOC of No.11 Group respectively.

**Did you know?**

Fighter Command lost 544 aircrew in the Battle, and a further 422 were injured.

*Flying Officer P.R-F. Burton of No.249 Squadron, one of 'The Few' who gave his life.*

for their aircraft, bursting through the inscription, 'The Battle of Britain'.

Accompanying them are bronze plaques holding in raised relief the names of the 2,936 aircrew of Fighter Command who flew in the Battle of Britain, grouped under their respective countries. The plaques also incorporate a short description of the events, the badges of the Fighter Command squadrons involved, and, facing the adjacent RAF Memorial, the badge of Fighter Command. The plinth beneath the relief is engraved with Sir Winston Churchill's famous phrase, 'Never in the field of human conflict was so much owed by so many to so few.'

**Did you know?**

The Southern Railway created a Battle of Britain class of steam engine. Names included *Fighter Command, Lord Dowding, Sir Keith Park, Biggin Hill* and various aircraft and squadrons that had taken part in the Battle.

*The Battle of Britain Class locomotive 602 Squadron.*

*The Battle of Britain Memorial on London's Embankment.*

A relief of anti-aircraft gunners on the Embankment memorial.

**Did you know?**

All aircrew who flew operationally with Fighter Command are entitled to the clasp 'Battle of Britain' on the 1939–45 Star.

*The medal group of Squadron Leader 'Buck' Casson includes the 1939–45 Star with the 'Battle of Britain' clasp.*

# THE FEW

'Mac' Mackenzie, 501 Squadron.

Paul Webb, 602 Squadron.

*Mike Cooper-Slipper, 605 Squadron.*

*Ben Bennions, 41 Squadron.*

*Pete Brothers, 32 and 257 Squadrons.*

*Bill Blackadder, 607 Squadron.*

Don Kingaby, 266 and 92 Squadrons.

Tom Dalton-Morgan, 43 Squadron.

*Mike Stephens, 232 Squadron.*

*Bob Stanford Tuck, 92 and 257 Squadrons.*

*'Hawkeye' Wells, 266 Squadron.*

*Ivor Cosby, 610 and 72 Squadrons.*

'Cocky' Dundas, 616 Squadron.

'Buck' Casson, 616 Squadron.

Ken Holden, 616 Squadron.

# BATTLE OF BRITAIN MILESTONES

*A Heinkel He 59 shot down by an Anson pilot of a No.217 Squadron near the Channel Islands on 11 July 1940.*

**10 July** – The Battle is considered to have started on this date. For the next few weeks most German attacks were against convoys and ports, particularly on the south and east coasts.

**29 July** – The Air Ministry issued a communiqué that enemy aircraft bearing civilian or Red Cross markings would be engaged, unless their sorties abided by the Red Cross Convention.

**1 August** – Enemy aircraft raiding the West Country scattered leaflets with Hitler's message 'Last Appeal to Reason'.

**8 August** – Battle of Convoy CW9; intense fighting over the Channel, particularly off the Isle of Wight.

**11 August** – Battle of Portland; the RAF beats off attacks on the Portland naval base, but suffers heavy casualties.

**12 August** – First raids on RAF fighter airfields and radar stations while maintaining

pressure against shipping and harbours. The CH radar site at Ventnor on the Isle of Wight was put out of action.

**13 August** – *Adler Tag*, the day on which, according to the German plans, Fighter Command should have been severely damaged. The Luftwaffe flew its greatest number of sorties to date – 1,485.

◄ *A milkman 'enjoys' Hitler's Last Appeal.*

◄ *A hangar destroyed at Middle Wallop.*

*The remains of a Heinkel He III.*

**15 August** – Heavy raids by all three *Luftflotten*. Dubbed 'Black Thursday', the Luftwaffe suffered severe losses.

**16 August** – In an action over Southampton, Flight Lieutenant James Nicolson of No.249 Squadron earned the Victoria Cross, the only such award to Fighter Command.

**18 August** – Fighter Command's 'Hardest Day'. The Luftwaffe launched major attacks on the airfields at Biggin Hill and Kenley.

**24 August** – The crucial phase of the Battle commenced, with heavy attacks against airfields in the south-east.

**25 August** – Bomber Command sent 103 bombers on operations, with approximately half attacking Berlin as a reprisal for the Luftwaffe raid on London the previous night.

*Luftwaffe bombers make a low-level bombing attack against Kenley.*

123

**28 August** – First major raid against Liverpool, the first of four consecutive night raids.

**30 August** – Heavy attacks against the south-east airfields.

**31 August** – Fighter Command suffered its heaviest losses to date.

**1 September** – Four main attacks on Fighter Command airfields caused heavy damage.

**7 September** – Pressure on the fighter airfields eased as the Luftwaffe switched to bombing London with a massed attack.

**11 September** – Hitler postponed Operation Sealion until 14 September.

**15 September** – The last large daylight attack on London. Highest German losses since 18 August. Later, this date became Battle of Britain Day.

**16 September** – Goering conferred on the losses of the previous day and decided to return to a policy of attacking Fighter Command.

**19 September** – Hitler ordered a stop to the final assembly of the invasion fleet.

**24 September** – The Supermarine works at Southampton was attacked and wrecked.

**1 October** – A third of the German fighter force – 250 aircraft – was converted to fighter-bomber duties, with the Germans

*◄ Shot down Luftwaffe aircrew pass through London en-route to a POW camp.*

beginning to reserve their bombers for night attacks.

**12 October** – Hitler decided to postpone Operation Sealion until the spring or early summer of 1941.

**25 October** – The Italian Air Force flew its first operations when 16 aircraft were sent to bomb Harwich. The raid was ineffective.

**26 October** – The last significant daylight bombing raids against London were mounted.

**31 October** – The official end of the Battle.

## BATTLE OF BRITAIN

Bekker, Cajus, *The Luftwaffe War Diaries,* MacDonald, 1964

Bishop, Patrick, *Battle of Britain, A Day-by-Day Chronology,* Quercus, 2009

James, T.C.G., *The Battle of Britain, Air Defence of Great Britain,* Cass, 2000

Mason, Francis, *The Battle over Britain,* RAF Museum, 1990

Nesbitt, Roy Conyers, *The Battle of Britain,* Sutton, 2000

Ramsay, William G., *The Battle of Britain, Then and Now,* Battle of Britain Prints, 1989

Simpson, Geoff, *A Dictionary of the Battle of Britain,* Halsgrove, 2009

Wood & Dempster, *The Narrow Margin,* Arrow Books, 1969

Wynn, Kenneth, *Men of the Battle of Britain,* CCB Associates, 1999


## PERSONAL ACCOUNTS

Baker, David, *Adolph Galland,* Windrow & Greene, 1996

Bishop, Patrick, *Fighter Boys,* Viking, 2003

Deere, Alan C., *Nine Lives,* Hodder & Stoughton, 1959

Dundas, Hugh, *Flying Start,* Stanley Paul, 1988

Forrester, Larry, *Fly for Your Life, The Story of the Immortal Tuck,* Muller, 1956

Galland, Adolf, *The First and The Last,* Methuen & Co., 1955

Gray, Colin, *Spitfire Patrol,* Hutchinson, 1990

Hillary, Richard, *The Last Enemy,* Macmillan, 1950

Kent, J.A., *One of the Few*, William Kimber, 1971

Kesselring, Albert, *The Memoirs of Field Marshal Kesselring*, Greenhill, 1988

Kingcome, Brian, *A Willingness to Die*, Tempus, 1999

Lucas, Laddie, *Flying Colours, The Epic Story of Douglas Bader*, Hutchinson, 1981

Orange, Vincent, *Sir Keith Park*, Methuen, 1984

Orange, Vincent, *Dowding of Fighter Command*, Grub Street, 2008

Page, Geoffrey, *Shot Down in Flames*, Grub Street, 1999

Smith, Duncan, *Spitfire into Battle*, John Murray, 1981

Stokes, Doug, *Paddy Finucane, Fighter Ace*, William Kimber, 1983

Townsend, Peter, *Duel of Eagles*, George Weidenfeld, 1970

Vincent, S.F., *Flying Fever*, Jarrolds, 1972

Walker, Oliver, *Sailor Malan*, Cassell, 1953

Wellum, Geoffrey, *First Light*, Viking, 2002